FROM TRAGEDY TO WORKING STRATEGIES

Turning Your Traumatic Events Into Empowering Moments

TWYLIA G. REID

#1 Best Selling Multi-Award-Winning Author of Broken Wings

FROM TRAGEDY TO WORKING STRATEGIES

Copyright © 2019 by *Twylia G. Reid*

Biblical verses are taken from the New International Version (NIV) & The Amplified Version (AMP) of The Bible

Published by When Heaven Speaks, LLC

Post Office Box 55

Pooler, GA 31322 www.twyliareid.com

All rights reserved. No part of this book may be reproduced, stored in a retrieval system or transmitted in any form or by any means, electronic, mechanical, including photocopying, recording, or by any information storage or retrieval system, without permission in writing from the publisher.

FROM TRAGEDY TO WORKING STRATEGIES: Turning Your Traumatic Events Into Empowering Moments

1st Print Edition *Twylia G. Reid*

ISBN: 978-0-578-57573-5

Printed in the United States of America

FIRST PRINT EDITION

DISCLAIMER

All material in this book is provided for your information only and may not be construed as medical advice or instruction. No action on inaction should be taken based solely on the contents of this information; instead, readers should consult appropriate health professionals on any matter relating to their health and well-being. If you think you may have a medical emergency please contact your doctor or dial 911 immediately. The content in this book is not intended to be a substitute for professional medical advice, diagnosis, or treatment. Always seek the advice of your physician or other qualified health provider with any questions you may have regarding a medical condition. The information and opinions expressed here are believed to be accurate, based on the best judgement available to the author. Readers who fail to consult with appropriate health authorities assume the risks of any injuries. In addition, the information and opinions expressed here do not necessarily reflect the views of every survivor or caregiver.

DEDICATION

FROM TRAGEDY TO WORKING STRATEGIES is first dedicated to God who is truly the head of my life. I thank Him for giving me the vision and anointing to carry out the call upon my life to inspire other survivors of traumatic events as they travel their journey of healing. I thank Him for seeing in me what I don't always see in myself. I thank Him for stimulating my intentions and drawing my attention to reflect, examine, and react to His peace, presence, and power as I continuously express appreciation for Him allowing me to grow in grace and in the knowledge of Him as I continue to educate, empower, and enlighten those who come across my path.

Last, but certainly not least, to survivors of any kind of traumatic event no matter how big or how small. I dedicate this book to you. So many times people just don't know how to thrive after surviving a tragedy. They don't possess the tools needed, and simply choose to give up and throw in the towel. Not so! I am here to let the world know this as well as a few other things! This book is my gift of inspiration, encouragement, and motivation to say that quitting is never an option and that you too can go from tragedy to triumph!

I don't know what our future will be like but I know that God will be with us every step of the way.

Your Sister Survivor, Twylia

ACKNOWLEDGEMENTS

I must thank my family for all of their love, support, and prayers as I yet again set out to do what was mandated of me and write material that could be used for God's glory. Thank you again for their prayers, love, and continued support.

To my Friends, Readers, and fellow Kingdom Builders, thank you for allowing the vision God has given me to uplift and inspire you to expand your everyday use of spiritual disciplines! The love you all have shown me has been immeasurable and I truly thank God for each of you. You've made a difference in my life and I pray I make an impact in yours.

With that being said, I ask that you all continue to pray for me as I continue this journey teaching and empowering other survivors how to have the life they desire in spite of the challenges they face after a tragic event.

TABLE OF CONTENTS

DISCLAIMER iv

DEDICATION v

ACKNOWLEDGEMENTS vi

Introduction 1

Chapter 1 3
What If

Chapter 2 6
Don't Take It For Granted

Chapter 3 9
What About Your Friends

Chapter 4 13
Significant Emotional Events

Chapter 5 18
From Tragedy to Strategies

Chapter 6 23
This Too Shall Pass

Chapter 7 29
Perspective

Chapter 8 33
Appreciating The Big Picture

Chapter 9 36
Knowing Who You Really Are

Chapter 10 40
Personal Strength

Chapter 11 45
If You're Happy And You Know It

Chapter 12 49
Why Did This Happen To Me

Chapter 13 55
GOD Is In Control

"I Walk But Never Alone" 61
Affirmations For The Mind, Body & Soul Excerpt

ABOUT THE AUTHOR 63
Twylia Reid

INTRODUCTION

There are several common misconceptions that people who survive a traumatic event of some kind will never be able to have a productive life due to the extent of trauma they experience during the tragedy. This is so not true. Experiencing trauma is not rare. Everyone hopes they'll avoid the worst life has to offer—accidents, illness, loss or violence. Unfortunately, few of us will get through life untouched. According to recent PTSD research, about 6 of every 10 men (or 60%) and 5 of every 10 women (or 50%) experience at least one trauma in their life time.

Women are more likely to experience sexual assault and child sexual abuse. Men are more likely to experience accidents, physical assault, combat, disaster, or to witness death or injury. These traumatic events will unsurprisingly cause great anguish and sorrow. But it's not all bad news. Trauma can also be a powerful force for positive change! This book was written to help you do just that! That's right…you can have the life you desire in spite of the pain and suffering, the challenges, and obstacles you will face after surviving a traumatic event. Those feelings of helplessness and hopelessness don't have to become your daily dose of glimpses of what your life may become.

This book is a true story from my own experience, and

I hope you will find the content relatable, yet understanding that I am no expert but a survivor who has traveled a path from tragedy to triumph who knows the true meaning of "This too shall pass"! You will walk away with a better understanding of what it's truly like to turn your tragedy into empowering moments and become the strategist of your own destiny. My prayer is that this book will become a companion for you as you face whatever challenges, trials and tribulations that cross your path as you travel on this journey. Just remember one thing, you are not alone, even though you will have days when you feel that you are. If we were in this fight alone, any of the things we all have endured might have been enough to break us, but through it all we've been able to maintain because God is working in our lives. He just wants us to know that we can trust Him, and that His strength is indeed enough. ☺

CHAPTER 1

What If…..

What if, one day you were living your best life without a care in the world? You had an amazing job, great friends, and family who looked up to you. You were the epitome of what success looks like. Your life is truly grand! I mean, you've reached new levels of self-awareness and self-growth. This awareness has helped you discover interests you never knew existed which have paved the way to helping you discover new talents and, passions.

Your childhood dreams have manifested right before your eyes and each day you thank God for showering you with blessings you don't have room to store. You look at yourself in the mirror each day in awe of who you are and what you've become and how blessed you truly are.

You think to yourself nothing can bring you down because after all, you have all you've ever dreamed of having. Until…one day you wake up in a hospital room. Not only do you not know who you are, but you don't have a clue as to who anyone in the room is!

The people surrounding you kind of look familiar but, when they ask you what their names are you just don't know. They are giving you clues, reminiscing about things you all use to do or have done in an attempt to jog your memory. But, nothing is working and you become frustrated and afraid because you simply don't know what is going on!

There are several doctors, nurses, and hospital staff poking and prodding you until you just want to scream and tell everyone to leave you alone. After days of testing, testing, and more testing, the doctor finally reveals to you that you've been in a horrific accident and your life will be changed forever.

You feel numb, terrified, and shocked. Feelings of futility and uselessness consume you as you imagine what your life was going to become. Being thrusted into an unwelcoming situation and unforeseen circumstances was a journey you were not prepared for. All of your Christian beliefs somehow seemed to vanish and for the life of you, you just could not conjure up the lessons of faith you had been taught while living your best life.

You thought to yourself, "What am I going to do?" You truly had to dig deep and trust that God was going to make a way out of no way. After all, I know at some point while living your best life you heard someone say that, right?

FROM TRAGEDY TO WORKING STRATEGIES

Is this a scenario you can relate to? If yes, explain how it made you feel in the beginning. If no, explain how do you think you would feel if this were you.

_____
_____
_____
_____
_____
_____
_____
_____
_____
_____
_____
_____
_____
_____
_____
_____
_____
_____
_____
_____
_____
_____
_____
_____
_____
_____
_____
_____
_____
_____

CHAPTER 2

Don't Take It For Granted

It probably never crossed your mind that you may one day not be able to dress yourself, feed yourself, or do the things you've always taken for granted would be there. These daily routines are so ordinary and are always done without thinking twice about them. Something as simple as having a meaningful conversation is now one of the most difficult tasks you can perform. Not to mention tying your own shoes.

Several months pass by with each day filled with so much frustration and overwhelming emotions. You even begin to ask yourself and wonder what you could have possibly done for this to happen. You were living your best life remember, and were the one others looked up to. You begin to question God as if He made a mistake by choosing you. The anger you feel inside grows because in your mind you were doing all the right things you should have been doing so WHY DID THIS HAPPEN TO YOU!

You spend months in the hospital going through hours and hours of rehabilitation. Your body is tired at the end of

FROM TRAGEDY TO WORKING STRATEGIES

each day due to the rigorous therapy you endure. Your mind is mentally and emotionally drained as you deal with the thoughts that plague your mind of the tragedy replaying over and over in your head. No matter what you do you just can't stop thinking about it, you just can't stop asking God why you, you just can't wake up and say it was all a bad dream. You just can't! And, before you know it seconds turn into minutes, minutes into hours, hours into days, days into weeks, weeks into months, and yes you guessed it…months into years, before the simplest things start to become second nature. Well, that's if they ever do.

What are some things you've taken for granted in your lifetime?

___

After reading this chapter, have your feelings changed? If so explain.

___

Explain why one should never take things for granted?

___

CHAPTER 3

What About Your Friends

There is a chorus to a song that says, "*What about your friends, will they stand their ground, will they let you down again? What about your friends, are they gonna be lowdown, will they ever be around, or will they turn their backs on you?*" Yes, those same friends of yours who were around when you were living your best life. Where are they now?

Some may have gotten married and have families and children of their own. Some may have careers and now living their best lives. They don't come around anymore, not even a phone call. But you, your days are consumed with doctors, hospitals, clinics, and rehabilitation centers.

During times of crisis, we often depend on our friends for support. You'd think friends would draw closer at times like those. However, many drift away instead. Maybe it has something to do with the lack of regularly understood formalities for persistent tireless stress or nonstop heartache and anguish.

Believe it or not, most people do better with the finality

of a "*tragedy*" than when the "*tragedy*" isn't final or the stress is ongoing. What do I mean? Well, there are religious and cultural practices and resolutions for observing the passing of loved ones. People attend ceremonies or memorial events, send cards and flowers, make donations, and bring food. The same isn't true when the "*tragedy*" or loss isn't final or the stress is ongoing. There are no cards that acknowledge when an illness, injury, or family crisis becomes a continual challenge. There are no ceremonies for when a person's life is changed for years, perhaps forever. We have no customs for the grief that keeps on giving or the stress that becomes a way of life.

Some friends take it personal. They feel rejected and left out when they don't get included in the conversations and decisions about care and go away hurt or mad. Especially if the person is a close childhood friend who's been in your life for a very long time or a significant other. Some just may not be able to look at you in the condition you may be in. Some of your other friends may have an unreasonable fear of the diagnosis or problem and worry that it's contagious. Some may simply feel helpless to deal with their friend's stress, so not knowing what to say or do, they do nothing at all.

This result in them becoming more and more unavailable and isolated as you fight to restructure and redefine your life. Life as you once knew it has changed! The days are filled with stressors that cause anxiety and fatigues like you've never experienced. Most days you may not know whether you are coming or going…or going or coming.

You may be a young adult just starting to live your life searching for all the right answers and maybe even a way

FROM TRAGEDY TO WORKING STRATEGIES

out because now your memory, your vision, and your own physical abilities make exploring life on your own a safety issue now. So, you normally spend your time home daydreaming about what could have, would have, and should have been. You may be an older adult with a family, a career, and things you've worked hard to achieve and obtain in life. But now because of your restrictions and limitations, you can no longer function in manners needed to maintain which results in challenges and obstacles that hinder you from supporting and protecting your family they way you would like to.

You now find yourself in a place of unknown certainties and wonder if you will ever be the person you once used to be. Will your life ever be the same? You may have a caregiver who ensures your day to day activities go as smoothly as possible. This person is there for you when no one in the entire world is. When others can't do or won't do, this person will. Welcome to your newly adapted life as a survivor of a traumatic event! Now, this could very well be the life you live…but it doesn't necessarily have to be this way.

Do you consider yourself as a person who has lots of friends?

_____
_____
_____
_____

Who would you say invests more into the relationship, you or them? Explain your answer.

_____
_____
_____
_____

Do you encourage each other? If so how?

_____
_____
_____
_____

Name at least three of these friends you know for a fact have been there for you since you've become a survivor of a tragic event OR if you were to become a survivor of a traumatic event.

_____
_____
_____
_____

CHAPTER 4

Significant Emotional Events

What you have experienced my dear friend is a traumatic experience. In other words, you have experienced a significant emotional event that has impacted your life in major ways. The kind of traumatic experience that brings with it emotional and psychological reactions you can't explain.

Significant Emotional Events (SEE) are events with the capacity to change your perspective in life, your value system and, your view of the world! No matter whom you are what age, gender or race, significant emotional events appear randomly in everybody's life. You will be unaware as it surprises you and stimulates your inner being. It pushes you out of your comfort zone in ways you never imagined could happen. Its' impact is so noteworthy that it causes you to consider life and examine your personal values.

There are positive and negative significant emotional events. These include events such as marriages, the birth of a child or a job promotion. The negative events include things such as a traumatic experience, a separation or divorce, a critical illness, job layoff, or death. The significant emotional event normally makes you feel like your world is literally coming to an end. You may even feel like there is no future, no hope, no anything!

The pain felt can be deep and become literally embedded in your heart, body, and soul preventing you from thinking about anything else. The resulting emotions which follow this trauma can be trapped in your bodies. These trapped emotions which remain in your memories may possibly be the cause of many mental and physical abnormalities resulting in crippling and slow progress in your rehabilitation and recovery.

You may become complacent and totally unaware of it, but the negative emotions of hurt and disappointment trapped in your body could actually prevent you from enjoying a healthy life after a tragedy. Therefore, you must learn how to release these trapped emotions from your body.

In your subconscious mind, memories are permanently stored in the form of images, sounds, smells, tastes, words and feelings. You can redirect and attach these memories to something positive in your life by transforming significant emotional events into positive emotions. You don't have to drown in self-pity and misery. You don't have to live a life full of *what if's* and *if only's*. You know, what if you had of done this or what if you had of done that. Yea....*what if's* and *if only's*. You must learn to detach these emotions from the memories you have of the trauma.

YOU have to make a decision. You can decide to activate your *FAITH* by Forwarding All Issues To Him, or you can decide to walk in *FEAR*, False Evidence Appearing

FROM TRAGEDY TO WORKING STRATEGIES

Real. YOU have the power to decide! How can anyone ask for more? Great is the promise of the Lord to the faithful everywhere. How wondrous are the ways of the Almighty when we walk in faith before Him? Yes, you have to power to decide to walk by faith. You have the power to move forward on your everlasting journey, one step at a time.

What Significant Emotional Event(s) have you experienced?

_____
_____
_____
_____

After reading this chapter what are some of the "What If's" and "If Only's" did you think about?

_____
_____
_____
_____

What negative effects did this Significant Emotional Event have on you?

_____
_____
_____
_____

What are some of the positive things that manifested as a result of you persevering and pushing through this Significant Emotional Event?

_____
_____
_____
_____

FROM TRAGEDY TO WORKING STRATEGIES

Which decision did you make FAITH or FEAR? Explain your reasons for choosing the one you chose.

_____
_____
_____
_____
_____

CHAPTER 5

From Tragedy to Strategies

How do you deal with misfortune and tragedy? How do you recover from the challenging times when life just happens? How can you thrive when your life is disrupted and turned upside down to an untimely event? How you YOU…cope with tragedy?

I know it's hard, oh boyyyy do I know…trust me. I understand how these challenges can and will bring about unexpected and untimely hardships that cause you to feel like there's no exit, no way out. Well guess what there is! There are strategies available to help get you endure through the tough times after surviving a traumatic event. These strategies will help you maintain through the pain, and help you push through the pressure. You too can see how prayer, perseverance, and keeping your perspective are the keys to successfully travel from tragedy to triumph.

At some point in life every person on this Earth will either be a caregiver, are a caregiver, have been a caregiver, or is the loved one of a caregiver, the *survivor*. Ready or not, like it or not, this is something that will occur at some point

FROM TRAGEDY TO WORKING STRATEGIES

in your life. So, the question is will you be ready? My advice to you is this....YOU BETTER BE READY!!!

Tragedy and misfortune come in many ways. When it happens it normally disrupts your emotional, mental and physical wellbeing; making you think and behave differently. Sometimes tragedy comes in the form of death, natural disasters, illness, injury, or really a loss of any kind.

Your values guide your approach to life and associations. They inform your way forward through the choices you are presented every day. They actually make up a large part of who you are, and how others view you. So unless you experience a significant emotional event you are normally making conscious efforts to adjust your values daily to fit whatever you are dealing with in your life.

A birth of a child, a death, a marriage, a separation or divorce, an injury, or illness are all things that can wreak havoc in a person's world making them think, behave, and feel differently. Everything changes for that person, but the rest of the world continues, unaware to the internal turmoil and chaos they might be experiencing. One of the most important things you must remember when it happens is that you cannot run and hide. Traumatic stress is a normal reaction to a traumatic event but can also hinder your recovery and healing. When you stay silent it causes you to relive the event over and over again in your mind. Repetitious thinking or viewing horrific images over and over can overwhelm your nervous system, making it harder to think clearly. This causes the negative thought talk to continue in your mind without you realizing its happening. You can't become silent and quarantine yourself from the rest of the world.

The truth is there are actually people in this world who most likely have already gone through what you are going through or have gone through. Yes, they have experienced the same hurt you are experiencing, the same disappointment you are, and the same heartache and pain as you.

According to www.worldometers.info/world-population as of September 2019 the current world population is 7.7 billion people. The significance in this statistics is simply this… you are not alone! This is why you can't stay silent. When you start sharing your story with others you will find yourself connecting with others who have walked in your shoes. This will allow you the opportunities to come together with people and brainstorm to discover strategies and tools needed to assist with the challenges you both are dealing with. Realizing you are not alone is your beginning to your healing! It is the opening you need to help you break through the pain.

You will begin to see windows and doors of opportunities opening for you to live the life you desire in spite of the challenges you may be facing since your traumatic event occurred. Accepting these feelings and allowing yourself to feel what you feel, is necessary for healing. Allow yourself to feel whatever you're feeling without judgment or guilt.

Give yourself time to heal. Take all the time you need. Don't try to force the healing process, and don't allow others to rush you into dealing with life until you are ready. Be patient but at the same time be proactive with the pace of recovery, after all you are your biggest advocate. Speak up for yourself and don't be afraid to express your needs and wants.

FROM TRAGEDY TO WORKING STRATEGIES

When it comes to the strategies used to help you get on track so you can enjoy your life realizing that tragic events don't have to be the end of your life you'll see your life through an entire set of new eyes. You will see that no matter what may have occurred that you can undeniably live a productive life in spite of the daily challenges you face. You will discover it is indeed possible to turn your tragedy into empowering moments and become the strategist of your own destiny.

What are some positive things that can come out of you not hiding and staying silent, but sharing your testimony with others instead?

___

What are some negative things that can occur if you decide to isolate yourself from others after a traumatic event?

___

CHAPTER 6

This Too Shall Pass

This too shall pass! How many times have you heard someone say this? More than a dozen I'm sure. Well, there is a reason we were taught that this too shall pass. As a matter of fact let's just say it together. Ready, set, go, *"This too shall pass!"*

This is your reminder to tell you that although things may look bad, are hard to deal with, and may not look so good right now that it will get better soon. Sooner or later you will hurt less, the pain and heartache you are enduring will indeed subside, the lonely days and nights will soon be over. Brighter days are ahead! Yes, this too shall pass.

Realizing that life is constantly in a state of change, and in due time all things eventually do pass is one of the most effective mindsets to have. Life is always changing and evolving. Even around us, things that seem permanent such as mountains are actually going through constant changes as the unseen forces underneath move and reshape its size and structure. When things around you are going bad and it seems as if there is no way out and you just aren't going to make it is when you need to stop, think, rethink, and make a conscience decision to keep pressing forward. You must look at the circumstances surrounding the tragedy that occurred as something that is only temporary. This will enable you to see through a different set of eyes and say, *"Hey I know things may look bad right now but it won't be this bad always."* This allows you to see the situation, with all your fear and dread somehow eventually ending.

When tragedy bringing a loss of some kind happens in our own lives, we can be too quick to think of it as something permanent and eternal. We get caught up in how bad everything is going right at that moment. It might seem as if you're stuck, unable to move ahead. You expect to endure everlasting life changing effects. Now, I know there are instances where some tragedies do leave behind permanent affects but, it's still not the end of the world. Life still doesn't have to be dull and motionless. You don't have to live in minimality (I don't think this is a word…but today it is) ☺. This is why it's important to remember that this too shall pass. Bad moments don't last forever. Whether it takes days, weeks, months, or years, eventually circumstances and situations change and difficult situations and hardships get left in the past. Even if some of the changes are permanent acceptance becomes easier when you remember this too shall pass! Oftentimes that little reminder is just what you need to help you get through any difficult times.

What I am really trying to say is this you've got to keep your perspective. During these difficult times your perspective is what will keep you going. When you are on top of the world, living your best life, enjoy it but know that things can change. And, if or rather when it does, just remember, this too shall pass. When you are at your lowest point, all nights are followed by day; at your lowest moments remember also, this too shall pass. Outward circumstances and material things change! That's just the way it is. There's nothing that can be done about it. Perspective keeps us humble and hopeful, appreciating how circumstances can quickly change.

Now I'm no dummy, and I know many of you may be thinking, *"Well, 'this too shall pass' might be true about totaling a car when you're in high school, dealing with a bad case of acne, dealing with a bad breakup, or challenges of a slightly more traumatic variation; but, not for real life altering adversity."* So, what kinds of things fall into that category? How about sustaining a severe traumatic brain injury and becoming paralyzed in an accident? What about losing your spouse after 50 years or more of marriage? What about losing a child due to some heinous act of violence? Surely you never really recover from these kinds of blows, right? I know that's how we feel when we imagine these things happening to us. But the research doesn't substantiate nor uphold our fears.

Research was done on older couples who had been married for decades showing that 6 months after losing their spouse, 50% of the surviving partners experienced little to no symptoms of acute grief or depression, and only 10% of participants suffered from a chronic depression that lasted longer than 18 months. This is not to say the participating partner did not miss their deceased spouses a lot, but that happiness did return to their lives fairly quickly, and their grief was not as incapacitating as many people imagine it would be.

Another research followed people after they had become paralyzed in an accident found that the happiness of the victims returned to near their baseline pre-accident levels within months following the injury. It showed how they actually took more pleasure in mundane tasks and felt more optimistic about their future prospects of happiness than another group which was also studied those who had won the lottery.

Looking at these studies expecting these traumas and others, people regularly overestimate how devastated they'd be and how long their depressed state of mind would last. Do you ever stop to think about why the way we imagine our reaction to a tragic event normally never match the reality of how we actually experience and heal after one? You tend to think more about what did happen, than what did not happen.

After surviving a tragic event you must learn to look at things pertaining to your future and focus on the things that *did not* happen rather than all the horrible things that *did* happen. Remember the years to come following your traumatic event has to contain something. Those years must be filled with episodes and occurrences of some kind. And, regardless of whether those significances are large or small, negative or positive you must pull them out of the gaps. You may not be able to physically see how important those absent occurrences will be but keep in mind they will eventually matter and become the driving force behind you persevering and keeping your perspective in check. So, no matter what your circumstances, remember, THIS TOO SHALL PASS!

FROM TRAGEDY TO WORKING STRATEGIES

After reading this chapter, in your own words what does the phrase, *"This too shall pass"* mean to you?

_____
_____
_____
_____
_____
_____

Nothing in this world is permanent. People change, things change, conditions change. Time passes, days passes, as well as years. What are some conditions in your life that have changed since you've now become a survivor of a traumatic event?

_____
_____
_____
_____
_____
_____
_____

In your own words, how would you explain what *"This too shall pass"* means to someone just experiencing a tragedy?

_____
_____
_____
_____
_____

What examples from your own life could you use to show other survivors how things changed for the good and for the bad after experiencing your significant emotional event? (keep it in line with the concept of this too shall pass)

_____
_____
_____
_____
_____
_____
_____

FROM TRAGEDY TO WORKING STRATEGIES

CHAPTER 7

Perspective

Perspective is merely a particular attitude towards something. It's your point of view regarding a particular matter. It's the way you see something. If you think that rap music corrupt children's minds, then from your *perspective* record labels that promote rap music are bad businesses.

Tragedy happens to all of us at some point in our lives. It's just a fact of life. In many instances tragedy can disrupt and disorganize your professional life and send you into a spiraling, out-of-control, negative state that is sometimes difficult to recuperate and recover from. By understanding the importance of adopting a few coping strategies and how to use them within the context of your life, you can put tragedy in perspective and even begin to create the life you desire in spite of any challenges you may be facing. And believe it or not, before you know it you will begin to use your own tragedy to better the lives of others! Wow!!! What a way to turn your tragedy into triumph uh?

Finding your way back to life after a traumatic event

isn't easy but I promise you it's doable. You can't avoid emotional pain in life forever. It's through your experiences of it you will come to understand what it means to be mortal…in other words human. When tragedy strikes, and it will, as you travel through the range of emotions; anger, rage, despair, helplessness, and hopelessness, they may seem impossible to deal with. You may really feel lost to the point of no return. When your heart is breaking and aching you somehow have to find that inner strength to carry on. You have to try to stay with what you are feeling, rather than trying to escape the pain by other available means which could become detrimental to you and those around you.

No matter what you have lost in life, no matter what tragedy you've endured you have the power to begin again. The healing of your wounds, the rebuilding and restoring of your life may take a long time but it is possible to begin again. Will it be easy….nope! But, it can be done. The key lies in your ability to see things differently, shifting your perspective from what you may have lost to focusing on what you still have in your life. After a tragic event there is no room for pity and misery because life is too precious to waste. You need to accept that the world is full of chaos, disorder, and confusion and that life is unpredictable. Ok, you got caught in the midst of the storm. One whose wind and rain literally ripped your world apart, but that there can also be a calming period afterwards.

You possess the ability to experience joy and happiness once again. When you stop struggling, when you come out of your depressed state of mind, when you are gentle and kind with yourself, and take time to look within, you will come to know yourself better. This will open your eyes to realize that your life does go on and that it is indeed worth living.

FROM TRAGEDY TO WORKING STRATEGIES

After reading this chapter, explain in your own words what perspective means to you.

_____
_____
_____
_____
_____
_____
_____
_____
_____
_____

Ok, you've survived one of the worst things in life that could have occurred to someone. What are your plans from here?

_____
_____
_____
_____
_____

What is your WHY for the decisions you've made to keep moving forward?

_____
_____
_____
_____

What are some things you can/can't do now that you could/couldn't do before the tragedy occurred?

_____
_____
_____
_____

What are some things you can do to practice being hopeful?

_____
_____
_____

In regards to perspective, change stimulates different parts of the brain that improve originality and clarity of mind. You can start small by changing your daily routines. Name 3 things you are willing to change in your daily routine.

_____
_____
_____

In regards to perspective…why do you think you have been given this opportunity to survive and now share your testimony of hope and healing with others?

_____
_____
_____
_____

CHAPTER 8

Appreciating The Big Picture

After a tragedy strikes you will most likely be placed into the role of a survivor or as a caregiver. You must learn to appreciate the bigger picture and learn to live more mindfully and feel a stronger connection to the things that truly matter in your life. For the most part, we live our lives instinctively, seeing only what we're accustomed to see.

Every once in while you get caught up and get a wake-up call in the form of some significant emotional event that leaves you devastated and wondering what life is all about. This journey we all eventually take, whether we realize it or not is one that brings about life lessons you never forget. The journey, referred to by various names is actually a journey awakening. A spiritual journey is what I like to call it. I call it this because things like prayer, fasting, and meditation help you to become more self-aware while on this journey.

As you come to know who you truly are and live your life with a sense of connection to the fullness thereof, you grow wiser, stronger, and more resilient. This is where the appreciating the big picture comes into play.

After a tragedy you must be grateful to yourself for having made this journey. Going from feeling lost, broken, embarrassed, to where you are now today says a lot about who you are as a person. It says a lot about your tenacity and your ability to push through and keep moving forward.

The hard work you do when you get tired of doing the hard work you've already done is perseverance! Life is life. Remembering you aren't alone is critical to your restoration. You can and you will bounce back from your setback. Be grateful that God has found you worthy to be the one to show others if you can make it out then they can as well!!! Now that's a praise moment right there!

Appreciate the big picture! Accept that change is a part of life and come to terms with any circumstances you cannot change. A time will come when you will have to look in the mirror and realize no matter how smart you are, no matter how loving and faithful you are, no matter how resourceful you…you don't get to control this one! And, there are just certain things not in your control. So, surrendering it ALL to God is your best bet.

Keep the faith and don't give up. You've made it out victorious and now it's time to let your light shine bright. It's time for you to call upon the strength and courage you will need to face each new day. Finding strength beyond yourself will give you levels of peace you won't even be able to understand. Peace that surpasses all understanding! You have meaning on the other side of this significant emotional event. You just have to maintain until you get there!

FROM TRAGEDY TO WORKING STRATEGIES

What are some things in your life that currently make you happy?

_____
_____
_____

Explain why acceptance is important after surviving a traumatic event?

_____
_____
_____
_____
_____

What does finding strength beyond yourself mean to you?

_____
_____
_____
_____
_____

CHAPTER 9

Knowing Who You Really Are

Changing your perception of who you are after you survive a traumatic event is vital to your recovery. Once you start to realize who you are and most importantly WHOSE you are, you will start to look at yourself differently. You may constantly find yourself wondering, *"How do I reconnect with myself after a tragedy or find my way back to the things in my life that were fulfilling?"* Well that's easy…you have to look at the qualities of who you are now. Allowing yourself to be known to yourself in an honest way is the beginning of embracing the person you have now become after the tragedy.

Once your perception of who you are changes you will realize you are stronger than you every thought you could be. Perception is the way you think about or the way you understand someone or something. It determines the way you respond to something. Your perception in life is determined by certain things such as your past experiences in life, your morals, values, and beliefs. In short your perception is your reality! It's the way YOU see the world and everything in it. It's your life.

FROM TRAGEDY TO WORKING STRATEGIES

Once your perception of who you are changes many of the things in your life you were once afraid of attempting will no longer cause you to become anxious and apprehensive. Yes you're probably feeling overwhelmed and flooded with emotions about all you've been through. It's now time for some good ole fashion self-care. All the attention you once gave to others now needs to be poured into yourself. Use daily affirmations to remind yourself just how wonderful you truly are. Use power phrases like, "*I Can*", "*I Will*", and "*I Am*" daily to help strengthen your view of yourself. This will assist you feel more confident in your abilities to do things, and in your ability to make decisions for yourself.

Most importantly, once your perception of who you are changes you will start to love and appreciate the person you have become. All you need to do is take one day at a time without badgering yourself in the process. Encourage yourself, eat healthy, exercise as often as you can, and oh yea…don't forget to relax. Don't suppress your emotions, there are there to be expressed. Find healthy, productive, and constructive ways to air them out. Try journaling, painting, or even writing a book. Look for ways to share your testimony of hope and healing to help others who are now at square one on their. Your inspiration and encouragement may be just what they need to make the decision you did to not give up.

Never forget who you were before the tragedy took place. I am sure you demonstrated strength, vitality and agility. You were active and full of energy. You moved with a purpose. I am sure you demonstrated courage and wasn't afraid to take leaps of faith to do things others said you couldn't do. You must understand that at conception you were a winner. You were the one who sparked life into your mother's womb. You were the one who brought joy into the lives of your parents, grandparents, and others. At conception you were great, you exceptional, you were rare and one of a kind. The mere fact that you were born means that winning has been a part of your nature before anyone ever laid eyes on you! Now look in the mirror and say, "*I won!*" Now, go in the other room and high-five someone, or call someone on the phone and tell them, "*I won!*" They may look at you strange or ask you if you are ok, simply chuckle and say, "*YES, BECAUSE I WON!*"

FROM TRAGEDY TO WORKING STRATEGIES

When you look in mirror how do you see yourself?

_____
_____
_____

How would you describe yourself to others?

_____
_____
_____
_____
_____

Write down 3 *I AM* affirmations to tell yourself each day.

I AM _____

I AM _____

I AM _____

CHAPTER 10

Personal Strength

Being a survivor of a traumatic event isn't an easy task. You must always maintain an awareness of your own personal strength. Realizing it really took strength for you to step into this role as a survivor or as a caregiver of a survivor without a road map or guide lines is astounding all by itself. So what if you make mistakes along with way. Guess what, everyone does so it's no big deal. Keep patting yourself on the back speaking daily affirmations to remind yourself that you are indeed *awesome* and oh so *amazing*!

The personal strengths you own will often always manifest as behaviors, characteristics, learned information, or natural talents. They are what make you unique as an individual. They are what make you stand out in a crowd. Your personal strengths are a percentage of what makes you…you.

Several problems can arise if you are not aware of your personal strengths. For one, you will not be able to utilize them if a situation warrants you to if you don't know what they are. This can cause you to miss out on true fulfillment in your life and as the person you have now become. Taking note of your personal strengths simply means paying attention to the thing you like about yourself. What qualities about you stand out more than others? What sparks your interest? What makes you happy? What makes you sad? What brings you joy and peace? What makes you proud each day when you look in the mirror?

You must also be aware of your weaknesses when determining your personal strengths. It's just as important to know your weaknesses because they can hold you back from achieving many great things. Acknowledging your weaknesses reveal areas that you actually have the power to improve. Remember just because you have weaknesses doesn't mean you have to keep them! Knowing your own personal strengths and weaknesses gives you a better understanding of yourself and how you function. You will grow more, because knowing what you can excel at will enable you to achieve so much more than you ever imagined you could.

Knowing your personal strengths also builds your self-confidence. Believing in your own ability to succeed is very important. You must believe in yourself. There may come a time when others won't, and if this happens it won't hinder or slow you down because you will have the ability and courage to encourage yourself! This is another reason why it's so important for you to know your own personal strengths. Confidence is interconnected to doing! The more you decide to do, the more you attempt to do, and the more you actually follow through and do, the more you will convince yourself you are capable of doing. The more you can identify and name those things you like about yourself, the more confidence you will obtain resulting in increasing your ability to achieve things beyond your wildest dream. Now shout, "*CONFIDENCE!*"

FROM TRAGEDY TO WORKING STRATEGIES

After reading this chapter, explain why it's important to know your personal strengths and weaknesses.

_____
_____
_____
_____
_____

What are 3 of your greatest strengths? (Be specific)

1. _____
2. _____
3. _____

Name 3 weaknesses that you have? (Be specific)

1. _____
2. _____
3. _____

What are some things you get complimented on the most?

_____
_____
_____
_____

What are some things you like most about yourself?

_____
_____
_____
_____

Go back and review all your responses. NOW…explain how you see yourself when you look in mirror!

_____
_____
_____
_____
_____
_____
_____

CHAPTER 11

If You're Happy And You Know It

Yes, you are a survivor of a traumatic event OR you are a caregiver of a survivor of a traumatic event. The world has not stopped nor has it come to an end. Concentrate on the happy things that are going on in your life. Each day you need to think about the things in your life that currently bring you joy and happiness. It may be a special relationship, it may be the new amazing friends you've acquired on this journey, it may be the smell of your favorite cupcake fresh out the oven, or like me it could be your faith. Whatever it is, try to find happiness in each day you wake up and be grateful for the life you have now!

It's ok to remember the bad...I mean you really can't just act like that significant emotional event never occurred. Just don't dwell on it. Don't become a loiterer in your mind and sit around each day waiting around pointlessly and idly without apparent purpose. Remembering the bad will help you refine and deepen gratefulness. It helps us not to take things for granted. In other words, if you want to practice gratitude simply remember the bad. The place you once were when your journey began. How you felt sorry for yourself and thought your life was over. How you fought hard each day to regain the use of your mind so you wouldn't fall into a pit of depression. Think of all the horrible times in your life, your losses, your sorrows, your heartaches and pain, the lonely days and nights, the countless tears you shed. Now, remember that you are here *now* alive and living with a purpose. You're able to remember the bad but yet celebrate the good times. You made it through those times; you made it through the trauma, you made it through the abuse, you no longer take life for granted to include the simple things you are able to do. You appreciate life and all it has to offer in spite of the challenges you may be facing. Yes…practice gratitude by remembering the bad!

Keep in mind all you have learned from going through these difficulties. Think about how you are now *qualified* and *equipped* to go out and help others who are traveling the same road you are on. You *can* and you *will* now use what you have learned to create a sense of purpose for others God allows to cross your path. This will help you keep applying an optimistic meaning to whatever happened in your life. Something meaningful and something bright! Even if it's the worst thing that's ever happened to you…keep practicing gratitude.

You may not realize this, but you can actually train your brain to be positive. While we can't change our nature, we can indeed train our brains to be more positive. Teaching yourself to become more grateful can make a huge difference in your overall happiness. Relationships are one of the biggest sources of happiness in our lives. And as you become happier, you will attract more people and healthier relationships, leading to even greater positivity and enjoyment. I guess you could say happiness is the gift that

FROM TRAGEDY TO WORKING STRATEGIES

keeps on giving.

Make a conscience effort to stay connected to the people who make your life brighter. Those who bring positive vibes only! Stay away from people who talk negative and try to keep you in a state of depression. You've come a long way baby….and you aren't going backwards. Not today, no way, no how! You'll be happier for it. Prayer and meditation are powerful tools for learning to live in and enjoy the moment. And you don't have to be religious or even spiritual to reap its benefits. Simply praying, speaking words and meditation is exercise for your brain. When done on a regular basis, positive words said aloud appear to decrease activity in the areas of the brain associated with negative thoughts, anxiety, and depression. At the same time, it increases activity in the areas associated with joy, satisfaction, and peace. It also strengthens areas of the brain in charge of managing emotions and controlling attention. This will help you become fully engaged in your present state of being and more aware and thankful of good things. Go figure! Daily prayer and meditation is not only good for the mind, body, and soul, it's also great for the brain! Who'd of thunk it! ☺

List 2 more things that bring you happiness.

1._____

2._____

List at least 2 really *bad* things that have happened in your life.

1._____

2._____

From those two events list at least 3 *good* things that came out of each one.

1._____

2._____

3._____

1._____

2._____

3._____

FROM TRAGEDY TO WORKING STRATEGIES

CHAPTER 12

Why Did This Happen To Me

Applying a defining meaning to the tragedy is the last step in turning your tragedy into empowering moments. It's one of the most important steps in this process. Thinking about how this tragedy has made you better and not bitter and how your journey of hope and healing will now change lives around the world is a moment of *AWE* all by itself.

The Bible tells us that, *"David wept."* What does this imply? It tells us that even those of us in God's will are not exempt from hardships and tragedies. It means just because you are the apple of His eye you aren't going to have some obstacles to overcome or battles to fight. David gave us one of the best examples of what a positive mindset is all about. Scripture tells us that even in the midst of him sitting amongst the ruins of the city, he did what none of the others around him did…he encouraged himself in the Lord! He made a conscience decision to not allow the sting of defeat get the best of him. He could have cried and went into isolation. He could have blamed God and those around him for all the bad things that had occurred. But he didn't, instead he did something! He got up, dusted himself off and trusted God to make a way out of no way. You see the very thing that was supposed to take you out God can use it increase you and take you to a whole new level of victory…just like He did for David.

We all know that life is more than a moment. It is made up of many experiences. Your life is an untold adventure of ups and downs, victories and defeats, good times and bad. But there are those portraits that forever capture and imprint upon your heart particular events throughout your life. They are called defining moments. They are moments in time that are branded into the fabric of your history FOREVER.

We know that we are at a defining moment in our life when our choices are about pleasing God and not pleasing ourselves. We know that we are at a defining moment in our life when it is faith that dictates our decision rather than reasoning and logic. Believe it or not there are several survivors of traumatic events who have difficulty experiencing defining moments in their lives because they can't let faith control them. They find it hard to do so because it doesn't seem logical to them. What do I mean? They can't see the light at the end of the tunnel because they keep holding on to the challenges and hardships they endured at the onset of their significant emotional event. This pushes them so far into a state of depression which causes them to lose hope of anything positive ever happening for them again.

There are two things about defining moments that are true; first, you are not limited to just one defining moment in your life and second defining moments will have a huge impact upon your life when they happen. Most likely, once

FROM TRAGEDY TO WORKING STRATEGIES

you have a defining moment you are never the same again.

We all have moments that have defined who and what we are. A defining moment in my life was when I became a mom. A defining moment in my life was when I became a wife. A defining moment in my life was when I accepted Jesus into my life and made Him my Savior and Lord. A defining moment in my life was when God called me into ministry. A defining moment in my life was when I joined the US Army and when I retired after 20 years. A Defining moment in my life is when I became a grandmother. Another defining moment in my life was when I wrote my very first book which is now a #1 best-selling book amongst other best-selling books I have written that are now empowering others and changing lives all around the world. One of the most life-changing defining moments in my life was when I became the caregiver to my son who sustained a severed traumatic brain injury (one of my significant emotional events) when he was only 11 years old. My point is this… many experiences have defined my life and have shaped me into who I am today. And guess what, so will yours!

Sit down and go inside yourself and do what I call a "*gut check*". This is a simple self-assessment to determine these things:

1. What lesson did I learn from the tragedy?

2. Was I awakened to things I had been doing?

3. Were my priorities in the right place?

4. Was I living a life pleasing to God?

5. What areas in my life was I lacking in?

6. How was my character?

7. Was this truly a tragedy, or an opportunity in disguise?

I know in hardships and tragedies it's hard to believe that anything good can ever come from it know this; you will indeed get stronger, you will become wiser, and you will become more knowledgeable. You will turn your tragedy into working strategies...someday, some way, somehow. When you do you will then be able to help others turn their tragedy into empowering moments as well. It will be in that defining moment that the journey you are now on makes perfect sense, and that God seems so real!

Once you begin to realize there was a lesson for you in the midst of your tragedy to teach you something and you give you a positive outlook on life that will be the beginning to your healing! Now go use the strategies I have shared with you to turn your tragedy into empowering moments so that you can become the strategist of your own destiny. Allow God to order your steps as you prepare to walk in your purpose.

We live in a broken world where bad things can happen even to Godly people. This can be anything from accidents, loss, failure, abuse or even death. In all of these things, we can still hope in Jesus Christ knowing that He has overcome your pain and trauma and can heal you of emotional and psychological hurt. Use those defining moments God has given you to share with others to demonstrate just how powerful He truly is. Allow others to see through you that He is able to do exceedingly and abundantly above all that we can ask or think!

FROM TRAGEDY TO WORKING STRATEGIES

Remember God promises freedom from the trauma and hurt that you may be facing or have faced since surviving the tragedy you endured. This means you are more than a conqueror! Though there is sorrow and grieving today, God brings mercies in the morning fresh and renewed. He brings healing not just to the physical body, but also to the mind and soul. He is indeed our Jehovah Rapha…HE who delivers us out of brokenness and makes us whole in Christ! Let your life be the change, the hope, the inspiration and motivation others need to see as you continue traveling your journey from tragedy to triumph.

After reading this chapter, explain why it's important to determine what the defining moments are from your tragic event.

_____
_____
_____
_____
_____

Now, in regards to your tragic event, what were your defining moments:

1. What are at least 3 lessons you learned?

   a. _____

   b. _____

   c. _____

2. What areas in your life will you now change?

   a. _____

   b. _____

CHAPTER 13

GOD Is In Control

GOD is always in control. Life may not be fair, but one thing about it God is fair. You can rest assure that God sees and knows everything you've been through in life. And, His dream is not only bring you out...but bring you out stronger and happier with a testimony to share with others to give them hope. Why? Because God is in control and in the end He is going to use all this for your advantage!

Remember the enemy always fights you the hardest when he knows God has something great in store for you. So if your tragedy was one of the worst things you've ever endured rejoice because that means God's got a blessing waiting that has your name all over it. So, don't walk around bitter, shake it off. Take off that victim mentality and take on that more than a conqueror mentality. Why? Because God is in control!

Isaiah 60:1 tell us, *"Arise [from spiritual depression to a new life], shine [be radiant with the glory and brilliance of the Lord]; for your light has come, And the glory and brilliance of the Lord has risen upon you."*

This tell you that if you want a new beginning and a new life, then you've got to rise up out of the negative mindset and trust that God will order your steps. Stop complaining and start rejoicing, stop frowning and start smiling, arise and make the most with what you've got. Why? Because God is in control!

God told Joshua to go in and possess the land. The word possess implies action. If you want restoration and want things to change in your life you can't sit around waiting for something to happen. You've got to be aggressive and take action. Get rid of that slave mentality, dump that pour pitiful me attitude and move forward. Don't allow your negative mindset to keep you from God's promises. You are a victor…not a victim! You must take the tools you've learned and do something with them. You must let go of the ashes if you want God to give you the beauty. The letting go is the action that must take place. It is your *arise* moment! Your weeping is only for a night, now it's time for your joy to come! Why? Because God is in control!

Even when the enemy comes and does his best to take you out, your attitude must be that even at his best it will never be enough because you'll still be standing strong. When your attitude changes the situations in your life will begin to change. When your mindset changes your language will change, and when your language changes your life will change. God has a great plan in store for you, just do your part. It doesn't matter how long it's been or how impossible it looks, victory is waiting on you. Everything you need is already in your future and we can trust that God knows exactly what He is doing. Jeremiah 29:11 says, *"For I know*

FROM TRAGEDY TO WORKING STRATEGIES

the plans and thoughts that I have for you,' says the Lord, 'plans for peace and well-being and not for disaster, to give you a future and a hope." Allow God's promises to encourage you so you can continually move forward. Keep praying and trusting Him. He says He will be right there with you to strengthen, keep and protect you. So, because God is in control, your circumstances will not overwhelm you, no matter how much you feel like they might.

I am so grateful for all God's promises about His sovereignty and power, because by holding on to them and praying and believing that God would fulfill them, He has helped me to endure and persevere in FAITH when I knew without a shadow of a doubt I could never have done so on my own.

Arise my dear sister or brother in Christ! Fear not as you travel this journey. Why? Because God is in control!

After reading this chapter, what is God telling you to do to possess your land?

_____
_____
_____
_____
_____

List at least 3 things God has done to prove that He is in control of the situations in your life since you've made it through your traumatic event?

1._____

2._____

3._____

Are you ready to *Arise* and *Shine*? _____

Give God thanks for your time is now!!!

Well…you've made it through the storm and the rain. You've been through some heartaches and pain. But, through it all YOU MADE IT!

You know have the tools you need to go from *Tragedy to Working Strategies* to create the life you desire after surviving your traumatic event.

No matter how challenging it may seem….never forget that you are AWESOME and OH SO AMAZING and that THIS TOO SHALL PASS!

I love you dearly, take care and may God continue to watch over you and bless you immensely!

FROM TRAGEDY TO WORKING STRATEGIES

"Fear not, for I am with you; be not dismayed, for I am your God; I will strengthen you, and help you, I will uphold you with my righteous right hand."

Isaiah 41:10

TWYLIA G. REID

"From Tragedy To Working Strategies"

Turning Your Traumatic Events Into Empowering Moments

Excerpt from *"Affirmations For The Mind, Body & Soul"* A Guide For Survivors of Traumatic Events

"I WALK BUT NEVER ALONE"

Today I walk slow, fast, high and low… but never alone.
My head is held high with the confidence of a king, assured that my steps are ordered by God.
For I know that without taking these steps, I can never move forward nor move up in life; so, I must walk and not stand still.

Today I walk slow, fast, high and low… but never alone.
Even if I follow others in the same direction, my steps are my own.
For when we arrive, we may not be in the same place because I walk with the Spirit; so, my walk is not a race.

TWYLIA G. REID

Today I walk slow, fast, high and low…but never alone.
Today I will walk by faith, not by sight.
Today I walk but never alone!

ABOUT THE AUTHOR

Twylia Reid

Twylia Reid is a native of Columbus, Mississippi who currently resides in Savannah, Georgia. She studied and obtained a Bachelor of Science degree in Business Management at Trident University International while continuing to work as a Human Resource Manager in the United States Army where she is a 20 year retiree.

#1Best Selling, Multi-Award-Winning, multi-published non-fiction Author, 2019 Trinity Nonprofit Awards Finalist, 2019 Blacks In Government Featured Speaker, 2019 110th NAACP Conference Featured Author/Panelist Moderator, 2019 Unspoken Wounds Women Veteran's Portrait of Personal Courage Award Recipient, 2019 ACHI (Strength

In Sisterhood) Magazine Woman of Achievement & Author of the Year Award Nominee, 2018 48th Congressional Legislative Caucus Featured Author, 2019 Winner of The Authors Show Health/Fitness/Wellness Top Female Author, 2018 Winner of The Authors Show Female Non-Fiction Author, 2017 American Book Fest Best Book Awards Finalist, The Huffington Post Expert Feature Series "Who's Who –10 Black Female Experts to Watch in 2018" selected, and the 2017 Indie Author Legacy Award Author of the Year finalist. She's the Founder/CEO of **Broken Wings, Inc.**, a 501(c)3 Nonprofit Organization, Founder/CEO of **When Heaven Speaks, LLC – Book Coaching & Publishing**, minister, speaker, group facilitator, and brain injury advocate. She is also the founder of **Broken Wings Brain Injury Empowerment Group**, an online brain injury support group, and the Founder/Executive Producer/ Host of the **Conquerors Café** on Blog Talk Radio.

Grateful for the support she's received, and passionate about her role as a Traumatic Brain Injury advocate and caregiver, she was inspired to write her first book entitled **"Broken Wings"** to help others understand the life of a brain injury survivor and his caregiver. She also published **"What Do You Do…When Caregivers Need Care Given"** as a resource for those operating in the role as a caregiver to those with chronic or lifelong illnesses. Educating, empowering, and enlightening others she shares wisdom gleaned from the years of personal and professional care-giving experience for maintaining your physical, spiritual, and emotional well-being while caring for others. Inspiring and motivating others is what she lives for. Teaching them how to turn their tragedy into working strategies to get results in spite of life challenges is her calling. Her mantra is "Aspiring to Inspire Others"!

FROM TRAGEDY TO WORKING STRATEGIES

She's also the visionary and author of her signature book *"From Tragedy to Working Strategies: Turning Your Tragedy Into Empowering Moments"*, *"Just Because I Have A Brain Injury Doesn't Mean…"*, *"SOARING By the Power of God" 31 Day Devotional For Spirit Filled Living*, *"My Journey Goal Setting Journal"*, *"The WORD, the Truth & the Light: Bible Study Notebook"*, *"A Survivors Goal Planning Journal: A Brain Injury Survivor's Guide to Goal Setting"*, *"Pray Believe Receive Prayer Journal"*. She is currently working on an anthology entitled *"Confessions of a Caregiver"* which will be released in November of 2019.

To learn more about her and her mission to keep "Making the Impossible Possible' please visit her websites.

Additional books by Author Twylia G. Reid

"What Do You Do…When CAREGIVERS Need Care GIVEN" Caring for Yourself While Caring for Others

"When Caregivers Need Care Given Journal" Personal Journaling to Reflect on Your Emotions as a Caregiver One Day at a Time

"Affirmations for the Mind, Body & Soul" A Guide for Survivors of Traumatic Events

"A Survivor's Goal Planning Journal A Brain Injury Survivor's Guide to Goal Setting

"The WORD the Truth & The Light" BIBLE Study Notebook.

"Pray Receive Believe" Pray Journal

"SOARING By The Power Of God" 31 Day Devotional

"GET IT DONE" To Do List Planner

"But First…COFFEE" Monthly Planner

FROM TRAGEDY TO WORKING STRATEGIES

We Want to Hear from You

If this book has made a difference in your life I would be delighted to hear about it!

Leave a review on Amazon.com

www.amazon.com/author/twyliareid

BOOK TWYLIA TO SPEAK AT YOUR NEXT EVENT

Send an email to: info@twyliareid.com

Learn more about Twylia and her son's journey of hope and healing at: www.TwyliaReid.com

If you would like to donate to help spread awareness about traumatic brain injury and the devastation it causes families please visit: www.brokenwingsinc.org

Follow Twylia On Social Media

Facebook Pages:
www.facebook.com/authortwyliareid
www.facebook.com/BWINC

Linked In: www.linkedin.com/in/twyliareid
Twitter: www.twitter.com/tgreid02
Instagram: www.instagram.com/twyliareid02

References

US Department of Veterans Affairs. PTSD: National Center for PTSD, Accessed 6 Sep. 2019. https://www.ptsd.va.gov

Worldometers. *Current World Population*, Accessed 6 Sep. 2019. https://www.worldometers.info/world-population/

Reid, T. & Davenport, N. (2018). *"I Walk But Never Alone"*. *Affirmations For The Mind, Body, and Soul: A Guide For Survivors of Traumatic Events.* Savannah, Broken Wings. https://www.twyliareid.com

Austin, Dallas & Lopes, Lisa. "What About Your Friends." *Oooooooo...On The TLC Tip.* LaFace, 1992. CD Retrieved 2 Sep 2019.

www.ingramcontent.com/pod-product-compliance
Lightning Source LLC
Chambersburg PA
CBHW050705160426
43194CB00010B/2010